T0016017

The fantastically feminist
(and totally true) story of the
ASTONISHING AUTHORS

THE BRONTËS

ANNA DohERty

wren
&rook

MEET the whole **BRONTË** Family

Patrick changes the family name from 'Brunty' (a common Irish name) to 'Brontë' to seem more posh! Brontë means 'thunder' in Greek.

PaTrick Brontë
1777 – 1861

Maria
1814 – 1825
Died aged 11

ElizabeTH
1815 – 1825
Died aged 10

CHARLoTTe
1816 – 1855

Tabby is the cook, the housekeeper and an excellent story-teller!

TabiTha
1771 – 1855

Adelaide & ViCToRia

BLACK Tom & TigER

MARia
1783 – 1821

When Maria and Patrick meet it is love at first sight! Maria is very well-read and loves books, a trait she will pass on to her children. Sadly she dies when the children are very young.

AuNT BRAnwell
1776 – 1842

Aunt Branwell is Maria's sister. She moves in to look after the children when their mum dies in 1821. She teaches them arithmetic, the alphabet and how to sew.

BRAnwell
1817 – 1848

EMiLY
1818 – 1848

ANne
1820 – 1849

Flossy

LiTTle Dick

keePer

1822

The Brontë family live in a house in a little village called Haworth, in Yorkshire. Patrick is a priest, and the front of the house looks over his churchyard.

CHARLoTTe

EMiLy

BRAnwell

ANne

KeePer

Stretching out behind the house are the moors, which the children adore exploring. Many people think moors are very lonely, cold places, but the Brontës love them! They write about them lots in their stories and poems.

1824

Soon it is time to start school! The four oldest girls – Maria, Elizabeth, Charlotte and Emily – are sent to Cowan Bridge boarding school for daughters of clergymen.

This is unusual. School is expensive and often only boys are lucky enough to attend. The Brontë girls are fortunate that their father cares about their education.

But imagine the worst, most horrible school in the world, and you might be halfway to imagining how awful Cowan Bridge is. The children sleep two to a bed and the water for washing in each morning is so cold it is sometimes frozen. The girls eat burnt porridge for breakfast, and if anyone misbehaves they risk some truly mean punishments.

The school conditions are so dreadful that Maria and Elizabeth fall terribly ill with infections that make them cough badly and have high fevers. Sadly both girls die.

After that, Charlotte and Emily are home-schooled back in Haworth with Branwell and Anne.

1826

The children are very isolated, being
stuck at home and surrounded by lonely
moors with only each other for company.
But they begin to be feverishly creative ...

Patrick gives Branwell a present of
12 toy soldiers, which the four children
use to create an imaginary world
called Glass Town.

Each sibling has their own
soldier, and each soldier rules
his own island.

BONaparte
(or Sneaky)

GRavey
(or Parry)

Wellington
(or Wellesley)

Based on the imaginary Glass Town, the children act out little plays and make up stories, poems, maps, illustrations, landscapes and building plans ... all drawn and written into tiny matchbox-sized books – the perfect size for the soldiers to read! The tales the children invent are very long and complicated, filled with lots of wars and love stories.

Charlotte and Branwell create their own kingdom of Angria, and write tiny magazines for its people, with articles and advertisements just like real newspapers. Meanwhile Emily and Anne invent the kingdom of Gondal – a land that is ruled by powerful women.

Many of the poems and stories the Brontës write when they are older are inspired by these imaginary worlds.

1835–1844

As the children grow older, they begin to work as teachers or governesses. But none of them enjoy it very much... Often their pupils are badly behaved and extremely spoilt!

The Brontës secretly spend their free time daydreaming and writing about their imaginary worlds and the characters who live there, or about their beloved moors.

MISS BRONTË

1845

Charlotte, sneaking around in Emily's belongings, finds
a secret book of poems that Emily has been writing.
Charlotte thinks they are amazing, but Emily is outraged!

Once Emily calms down, Charlotte persuades both her
sisters to work together to produce a joint book of poems.
The girls choose 19 poems by Charlotte and 21 each by
Emily and Anne, and write them out into a manuscript.

The sisters work at night-time, while Patrick and Branwell
are fast asleep. At this time women aren't considered
clever enough to be writers, so they decide to keep their
poetry secret ... for now ...

1846

But before long, the girls decide to publish the poems under false male names. They do this because they know that if the poems appear to be written by men, people will respect them more. So, each sister chooses a pen name using the first letter of their real name and the surname Bell. The manuscript is sent out to publishers ... and *Poems by Currer, Ellis, and Acton Bell* is published in May 1846.

1846

Inspired by the excitement of having their poetry printed in a book, the sisters decide that the next step is to each write a novel. Again, they work together late into the night at their dining room table – in secret. Patrick and Branwell are completely unaware that they live with three published poets and aspiring novelists!

Once they have all completed their books, the sisters write their pen names on the front and send them off to lots of publishers. They will need to check the post for replies each morning before their father does, or their secret will be out!

1847–1848

Jane Eyre, Wuthering Heights and *Agnes Grey* are published, and are very popular!

A year later, Anne has written another book, *The Tenant of Wildfell Hall*. She sends it to her publisher.

A rumour flies around the country that it is in fact the newest book by the author of *Jane Eyre*, which is now a bestseller. Lots of people are intrigued by the mysterious Currer, Ellis and Acton Bell. Some have even started to suspect they are one person writing under three names!

Determined to clear up this muddle, Charlotte and Anne decide to reveal to their publisher that they are indeed separate writers. This also means revealing that they are women.

Shy Emily stays at home to look after the house, while Charlotte and Anne bravely travel to London alone…

JANE EYRE
CURRER BELL

1847

The story of Jane's life, from when she was a little girl at a horrible school (… guess what that was based on?) to her job as a governess, where she falls in love with her boss… But it turns out he already has a wife who is ill and lives in an attic at the top of the house!

WUTHERING HEIGHTS
Ellis Bell

1847

Cathy is in love with two people: her dangerous childhood best friend and her super-rich neighbour…

Tragic and scary and exciting … there are even ghosts in this book!

1847

The tale of Agnes: a kind, sweet yet brave heroine, who works as a governess to dreadful children so she can make money to send to her poor family (… inspired by Anne's own experience of teaching!)

AGNES GREY

THE TENANT OF WILDFELL HALL

THE TENANT OF WILDFELL HALL

ACTON BELL

1848

The amazing story of brave Helen running away from her cruel husband with her young son and living as an artist.

Women living on their own, making their own money and leaving their husbands (even if they are mean), is almost unheard of at this time. Because Helen is so strongly independent, this is considered to be one of the first feminist books.

1848–1849

Tragedy hits the Brontë family again.

Branwell catches an infection and dies, followed by Emily a few months later. The family is heartbroken, but Emily's faithful dog, Keeper, is the unhappiest of all, and even comes to her funeral.

Sadly, Anne also falls ill and passes away in 1849. Her last words are, "Take courage Charlotte, take courage!"

1849–1855

THE BRONTË SISTERS LIVE ON TO THIS DAY

Charlotte publishes two more books – *Shirley* (which made the name 'Shirley' popular for girls) and *Villette* (the tale of Lucy Snowe, who travels to teach at a French-speaking school). But then she, too, gets sick and dies in 1855.

What a sudden, sad ending for such a brilliant family! But the Brontë sisters live on to this day through their incredible, inspiring books.

CHARLOTTE

Charlotte can read in the dark!

 She is the only Brontë sibling to be married.

As an adult, she is missing many teeth.

She wants to be an artist when she is young.

She writes daily letters to her best friend, Ellen, who she has known since she was at school.

She owns a fragment of Napoleon's coffin.

The first book Charlotte writes is called *The Professor*, but it is rejected by lots of publishers. It is only published after she dies.

She hates housework.

BRAnwell

He can play the organ.

Branwell has red hair.

He has a number of his poems published in local newspapers.

His real name is actually Patrick Branwell Brontë, but everyone calls him Branwell.

He paints a portrait of himself and his sisters but then adds in a big column over his own face!

Emily

Emily runs the household — she does lots of cooking, cleaning and ironing.

She is extremely shy, sometimes refusing to speak in public!

She can be found teaching herself German with a book propped up as she bakes.

She can fire a pistol.

She is the tallest of all the siblings.

She adores the moors around her home, nature and animals.

She is very good at playing the piano.

Her best friend is her dog, keeper.

Anne

Anne works for the same family for five years — this is the longest any of the Brontë children have a job for.

Like Emily, she has a dog — Flossy.

Her very first job — as a Sunday-school teacher — is when she is just 12 years old!

She loves going to the swimming baths and for donkey rides on the beach.

She plays the piano and enjoys drawing.

She is fluent in Latin.

She adores the seaside town of Scarborough, and she is buried there when she dies.

The Fantastically FEMiNiST BRontës

To see how brave, strong and fantastically feminist the Brontë sisters were, you have to understand what it was like to be a woman at the time they lived. It might be hard to imagine now, but in the Victorian era – when the Brontës were living – it was very difficult for girls to be independent. Women were not allowed to own their own house, vote, be a politician, go to university, divorce their husband or even open their own bank account. But the Brontë sisters were bold and daring – they were determined that their work would be noticed.

Charlotte, Emily and Anne's rebellion started young. Growing up, the Brontë children adored inventing their own imaginary worlds, peppered with royalty, famous leaders, politicians and explorers. In real life, all these roles were filled by men because women were considered too weak to do them. So in protest, Anne and Emily made all their most powerful characters women. When the sisters were older, the main characters of every single one of their books were female, reflecting their own strong-willed personalities!

The Brontë children were fortunate that their father cared about their education and could afford to send them to school. Education was very different from today. Schools cost money, so often boys' education was valued over girls'. This was because girls were usually expected to grow up, get married, have babies and stay at home.

Poor children could go to school if they were lucky enough to have a free one nearby. If there wasn't one, children were either taught at home or just skipped school altogether and started working from a very young age. Richer families sent their children away to school or had governesses to teach them at home. Often, wealthy girls didn't learn "intellectual" subjects like maths and science, but instead were taught more "creative" things like music, art or a different language – skills that would make them an attractive wife, rather than prepare them for a career.

As they grew up, the Brontë children all moved away to teach. Women having jobs was quite unusual for the time. Some girls worked until they got married, but gave up once they had a husband.

For women who did earn a living, jobs were quite limited. As girls were not allowed to go to university, they couldn't do anything that required learning special skills, like being a doctor or an architect. Jobs with authority, for example lawyers or police officers, weren't an option either, because women weren't respected enough. It would be difficult to work in the police force if no one took you seriously! Careers that involved lots of labour, like building or fishing, were also considered too difficult for women.

For working-class women, there were opportunities to work in factories, or in laundries, or to sell things at a market or on the street. For middle-class women (like the Brontës), teachers, governesses, cooks and maids were common jobs – basically, anything involving looking after children or the home.

The Brontë sisters loved writing and making up stories, but one of the reasons they began sending their work to publishers was because they wanted to earn their own living. Being a governess didn't pay very much, so writing books was a good way to earn some extra money.

The sisters published under male pen-names. In Victorian times it was extremely uncommon to find published female writers because women were widely believed to be less clever than men. The Brontës used male names so that publishers would not reject their novels purely on the basis that they were written by women. The Brontë sisters wanted their tales to be read by everyone.

Can you imagine how stunned the whole country was when the sisters revealed themselves to be female? No one could believe that these bestsellers had been written by women! Especially women who had spent their childhoods confined to the isolated, lonely, windswept moors of Haworth. The Brontës hadn't experienced much of the world, but that didn't matter – their imaginations fuelled their amazing tales.

Nowadays, the Brontës' books are celebrated not only because they are brilliant stories, but because the writers themselves were so daring and unusual, creating such beautiful work in a man's world. The Brontë sisters truly are fantastically feminist!

For Scott and Pea x

First published in Great Britain in 2019 by Wren & Rook

Text and illustrations copyright © Anna Doherty, 2019
Design copyright © Hodder & Stoughton Ltd, 2019

The right of Anna Doherty to be identified as author/illustrator
of this work has been asserted by her in accordance with the
Copyright, Designs and Patents Act 1988.

All rights reserved.

HB ISBN: 978 1 5263 6106 6
PB ISBN: 978 1 5263 6107 3
E-book ISBN: 978 1 5263 6108 0
10 9 8 7 6 5 4 3 2 1

Wren & Rook
An imprint of
Hachette Children's Group
Part of Hodder & Stoughton
Carmelite House
50 Victoria Embankment
London EC4Y 0DZ

An Hachette UK Company
www.hachette.co.uk
www.hachettechildrens.co.uk

Printed in China

Every effort has been made to clear copyright. Should there be any
inadvertent omission, please apply to the publisher for rectification.

The website addresses (URLs) included in this book were valid at the time
of going to press. However, it is possible that contents or addresses may have
changed since the publication of this book. No responsibility for any such
changes can be acceptedby either the author or the publisher.